JUSTICE LEAGUE™

Doodles

Amazing Adventures to Complete and Create

Art adapted by Gregg Schigiel

RP | KIDS

PHILADELPHIA · LONDON

Books published by Running Press are available at special discounts for bulk purchases in the
United States by corporations, institutions, and other organizations. For more information, please contact
the Special Markets Department at the Perseus Books Group, 2300 Chestnut Street, Suite 200, Philadelphia,
PA 19103, or call (800) 810-4145, ext. 5000, or e-mail special.markets@perseusbooks.com.

ISBN 978-0-7624-4715-2

9 8 7 6 5 4 3 2 1
Digit on the right indicates the number of this printing

Cover design by Frances J. Soo Ping Chow
Interior design by Susan Van Horn
Edited by Lisa Cheng
Typography: Bulldog, Lobster Two, and Ziggurat

Published by Running Press Kids
An Imprint of Running Press Book Publishers
A Member of the Perseus Books Group
2300 Chestnut Street
Philadelphia, PA 19103–4371

Visit us on the web!
www.runningpress.com/kids

This book was created, completed,
and colored by

....

MEET THE JUSTICE LEAGUE!

MEET THE VILLAINS!

The Watchtower is the Justice League's headquarters.
Add more stars and planets around it!

Draw your own space station.

Superman can fly, bend steel, and shoot beams from his eyes. Show his heat vision in action!

A helicopter flies out of control over Metropolis.
Draw Superman saving the helicopter!

Batman is the World's Greatest Detective. He uses high-tech gadgets to solve crimes. Draw some clues to help him solve the case!

Look, it's the Bat-signal!
Draw Batman swinging across Gotham City on his Batrope.

Wonder Woman has bulletproof bracelets
and a Golden Lasso of Truth. Draw her Lasso in action!

Draw Wonder Woman training for combat.
Don't forget her sword and shield!

Superman, Batman, and Wonder Woman team up to take down a flying monster. What does it look like?

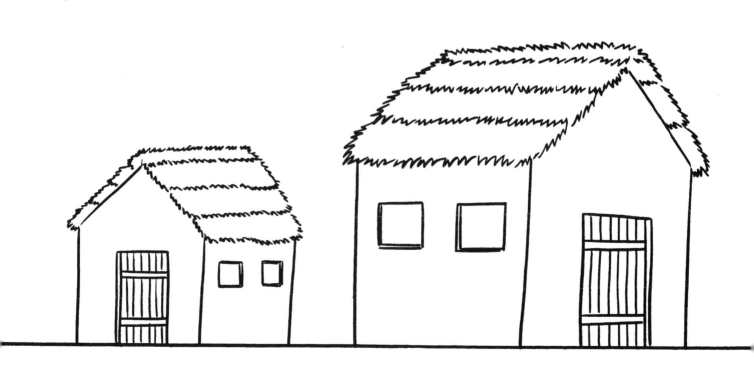

The Flash is the Fastest Man Alive.
Draw the villains he is racing
to fight.

Superman uses his freeze breath to stop Lex Luthor.
Draw the icy blast of air covering the villain!

The Flash runs so fast that sparks shoot off his costume!
Fill the air with electricity.

Green Lantern uses his power ring to create anything he imagines.
What would you create? Draw it here.

There's a kitten trapped in a tree! What would you create with your power ring to save the day?

Aquaman breathes underwater and can
communicate with all marine life.
Which sea creatures does he call to his side?

Aquaman, King of the Sea, welcomes the Justice League to his kingdom. Draw his castle behind him.

Martian Manhunter is a telepath with shape-shifting abilities.
Draw what he changes into!

Martian Manhunter flies over an alien terrain.
Draw the inhabitants. Are they friends or foes?

Hawkgirl is from the planet Thanagar.
Build a rocket ship so she can go back for a visit!

Help Hawkgirl soar into the sky and battle Star Sapphire.
Add Hawkgirl's wings. What does she have in her hands?

Martian Manhunter and Green Lantern guard the galaxy.
Are there any spaceships? Add some planets of your own!

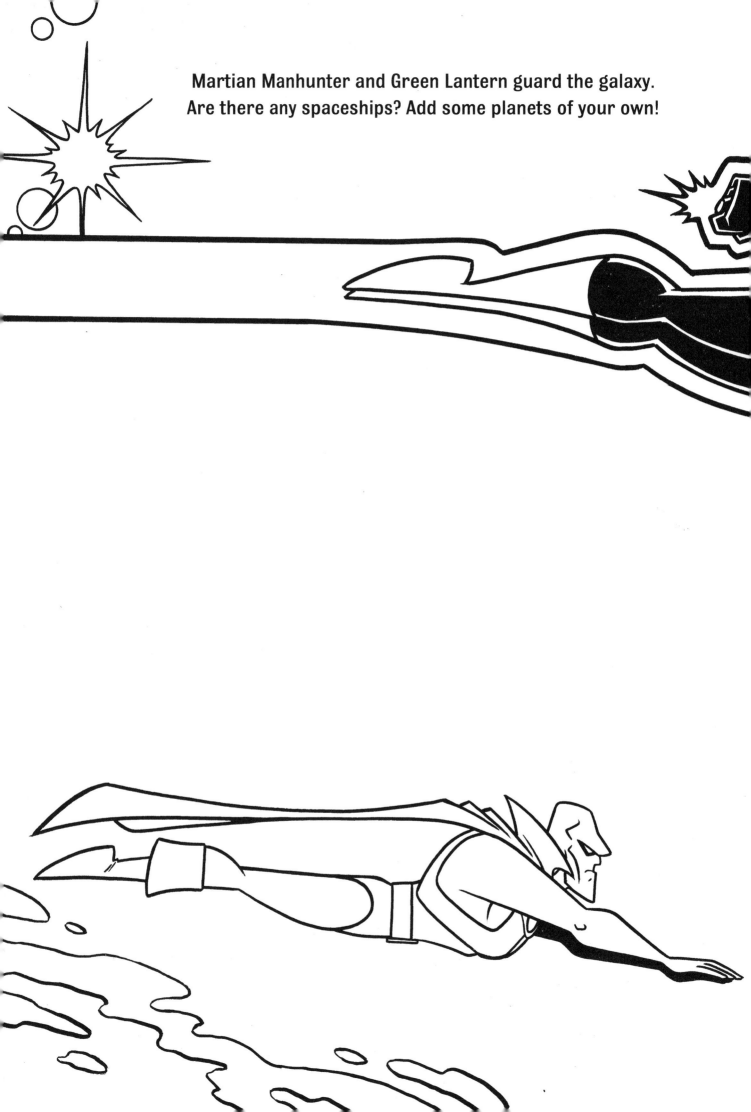

Green Arrow is an expert archer who uses a bow and arrow to fight crime. Arm him with his weapons!

Black Canary possesses an earsplitting scream that can shatter metal.
Draw the sonic waves in action!

Red Tornado is an android that can manipulate cyclones.
Show the tornadoes shooting from his hands!

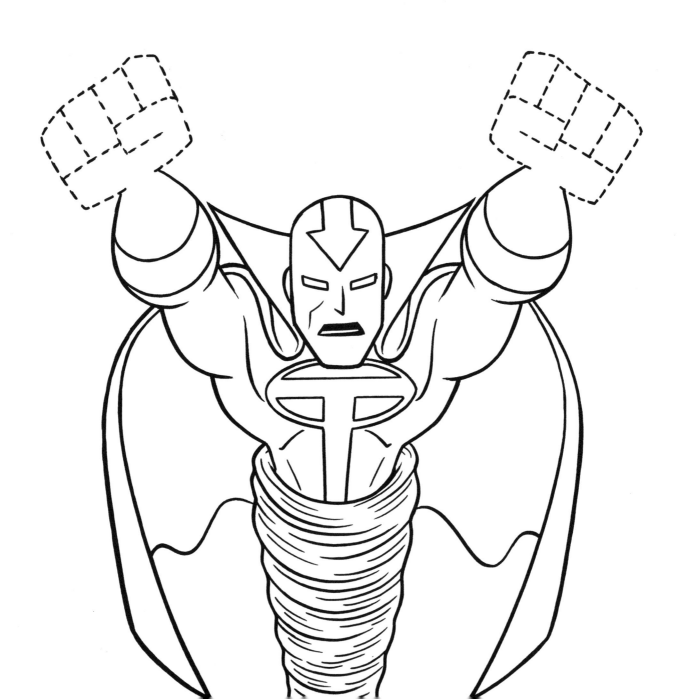

Wildcat is an expert fighter in peak physical condition.
Build a boxing ring around him. Who is his opponent?

The Justice League is trapped by Ultra-Humanite!
Help Elongated Man open the door.

Supergirl has the same powers as Superman.
What heavy object is she lifting?

Doctor Fate is a sorcerer with a magic helmet.
Add some magic words to help him blast fire from his hands!

Zatanna is a powerful magician and skilled illusionist.
What did she pull out of her hat?

The Mistress of Magic has vanished!
Help bring Zatanna back with your magical powers.

Zatanna and Doctor Fate combine their mystical abilities.
What do they conjure up?

Elongated Man can stretch his body to incredible lengths and sizes.
Bend and twist him all over the page!

The Atom is a brilliant scientist.
Help with the experiment by adding all the chemicals!

The Atom shrinks to a size smaller than a keyhole.
What is on the other side?

Congratulations! You're the Justice League's newest member.
Design your costume!

Does your costume have a mask or helmet? Draw it here.

Batman keeps gadgets and tools in his Utility Belt.
Draw your own gadgets. What do your tools do?

The Fortress of Solitude is Superman's arctic hideout.
What Kryptonian artifacts does he keep inside?

What does your secret hideout look like?
Are there machines, computers, and robots?

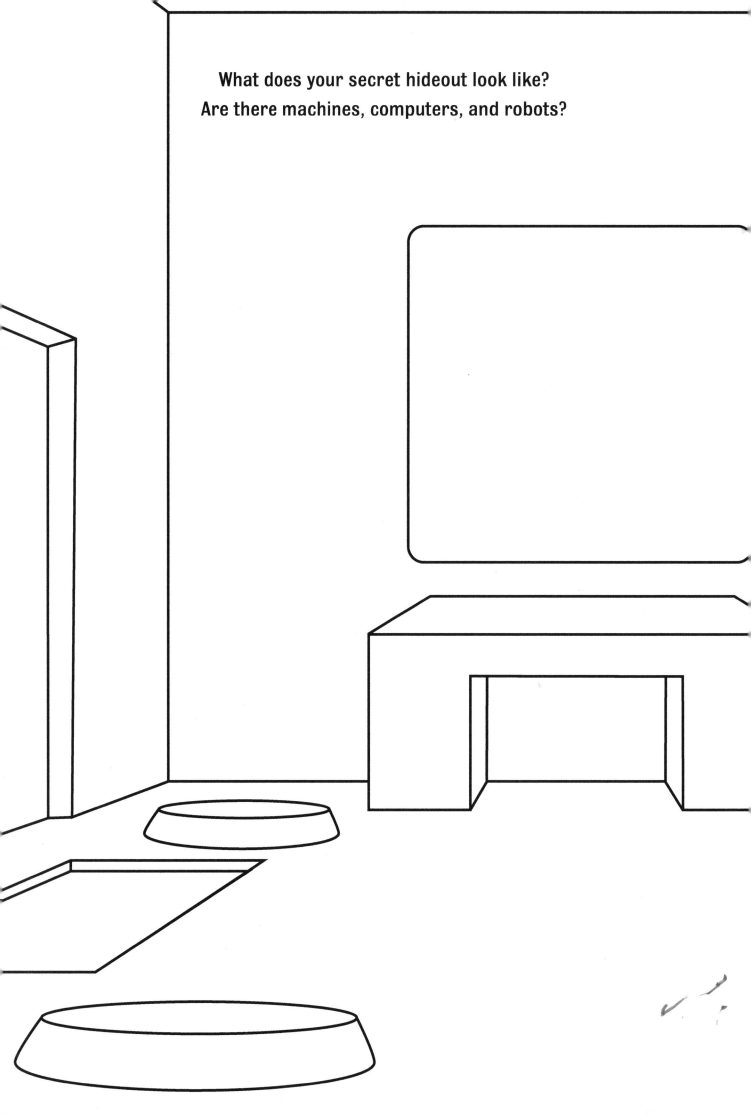

The *Javelin-7* is the Justice League's
mode of transportation.
Customize it with your artistic touch!

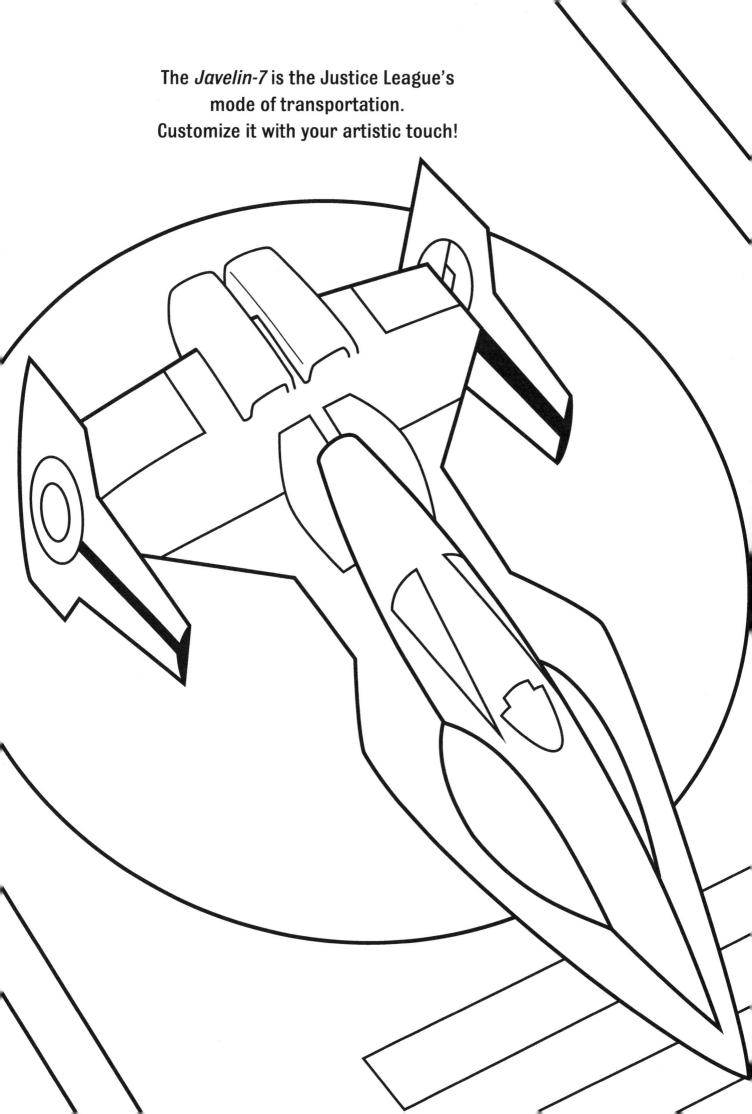

You'll need a speedy vehicle, too.
Does it fly? Does it swim? Build it here.

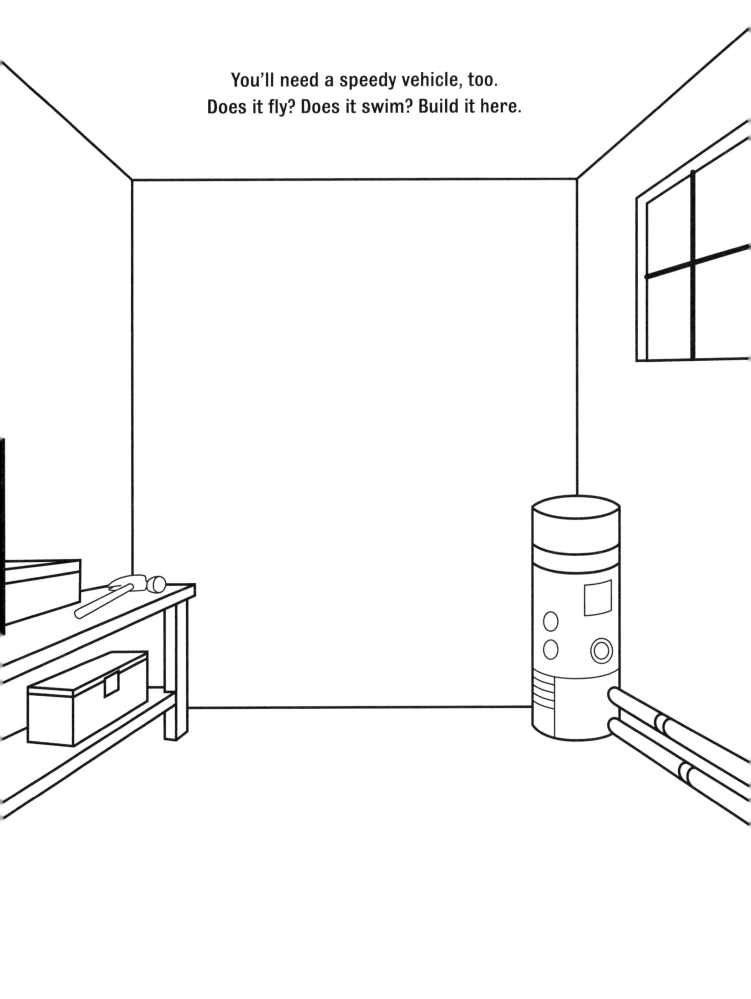

Draw yourself with your new costume and
vehicle standing with the Justice League!

There is trouble on Earth!
Draw your vehicle launching out of the Watchtower.

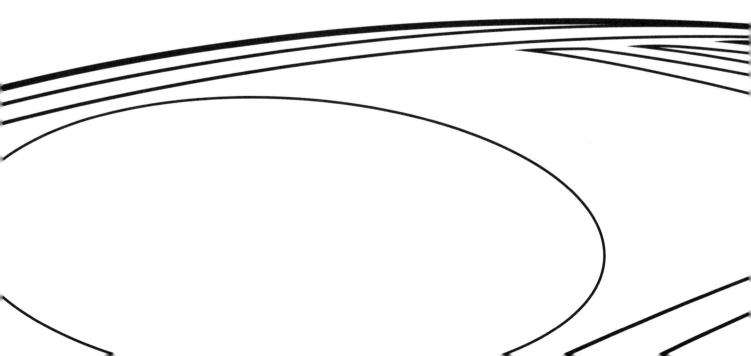

The Joker uses deadly party gags as weapons.
What kind of buzzer does he hide in his hand?

The Joker has prepared a trap for Batman.
Build the crazy clown's creation!

Villains have taken over the train station.
Draw the super hero who saves the day!

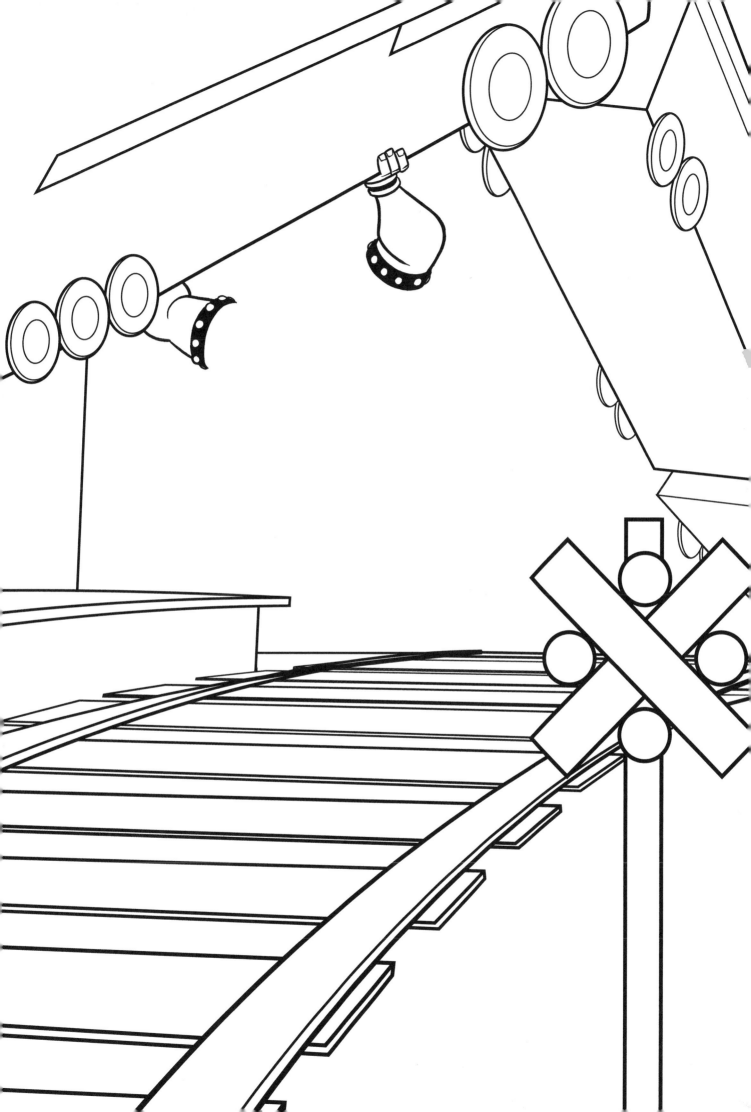

Gorilla Grodd is a scientific genius. He is creating an E-ray to turn humans into gorillas. What does it look like?

Grodd and Ultra-Humanite turned the Flash and Aquaman into primates! What do the heroes look like now?

Sinestro wields a power ring similar to Green Lantern's. What evil objects does he create?

Star Sapphire's magic gemstone fires intense energy beams.
Use the stone to create a force field around her.

Sinestro and Star Sapphire attack Green Lantern.
Their power rings explode with energy.
Complete the scene.

Lex Luthor's robotic battle suit gives him increased strength and flight. Is he a match for Superman? Color in the scene.

Brainiac has great knowledge of various alien technologies. He shrank your city and put it in the bottle. Draw it here.

Lex Luthor and Brainiac created a giant laser cannon.
Design it here.

Solomon Grundy is on the rampage!
Who will stand up to take him down?

**Mongul travels in an enormous spaceship on his quest to destroy Earth.
Finish his mode of transportation.**

Darkseid and Mongul seek to control the universe,
but the Justice League is the first line of defense.
Draw the epic battle!

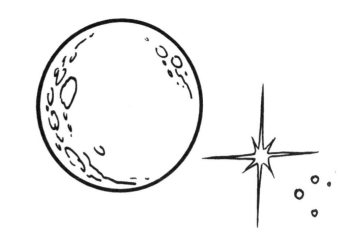

Supergirl is on patrol.
What is happening in Metropolis today?

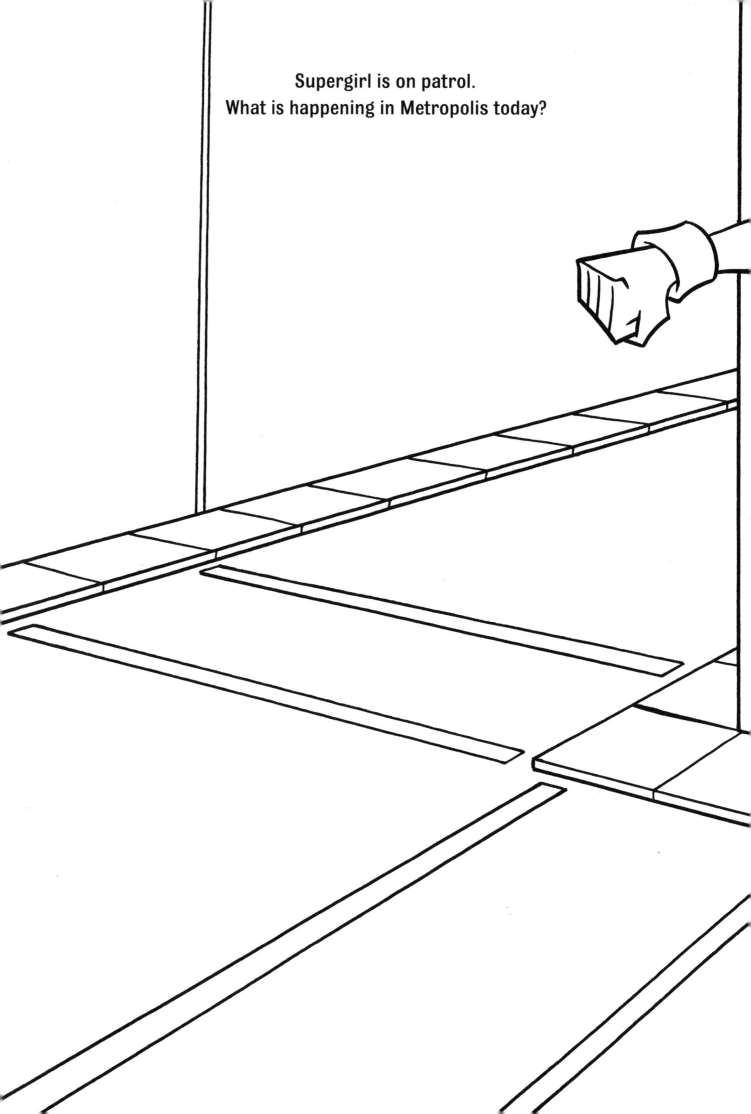

Amazo is an evil android that copies the powers of any hero.
Finish drawing the hero that was his last target.

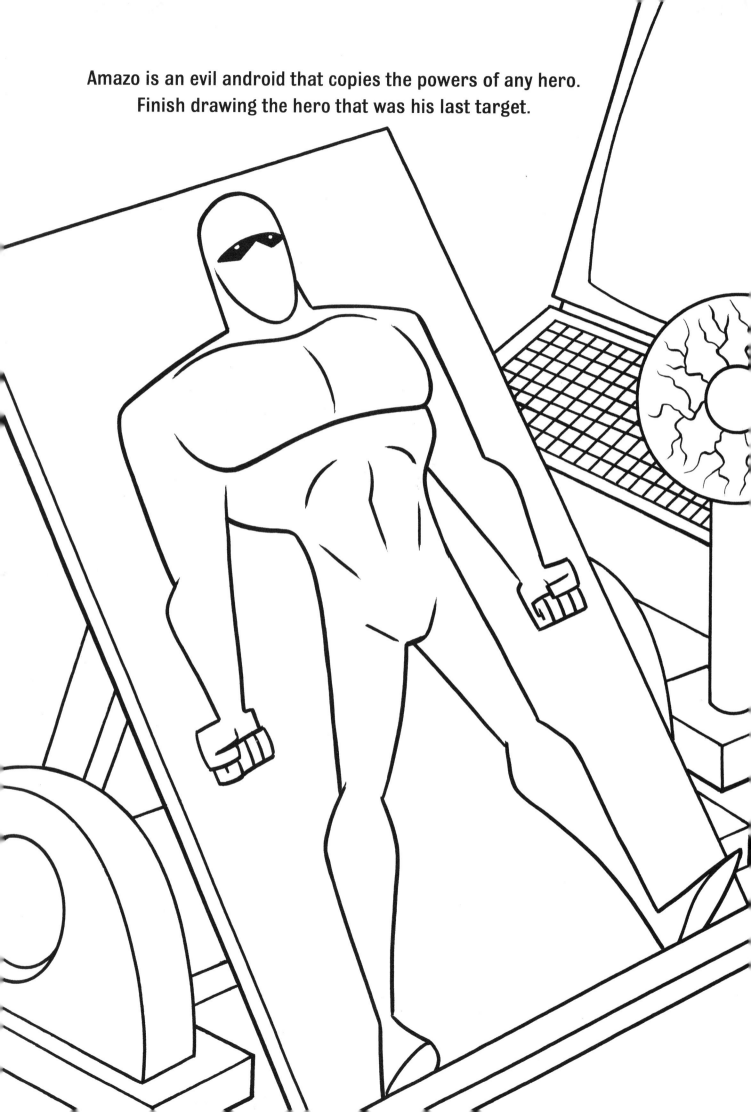

Build your own android!

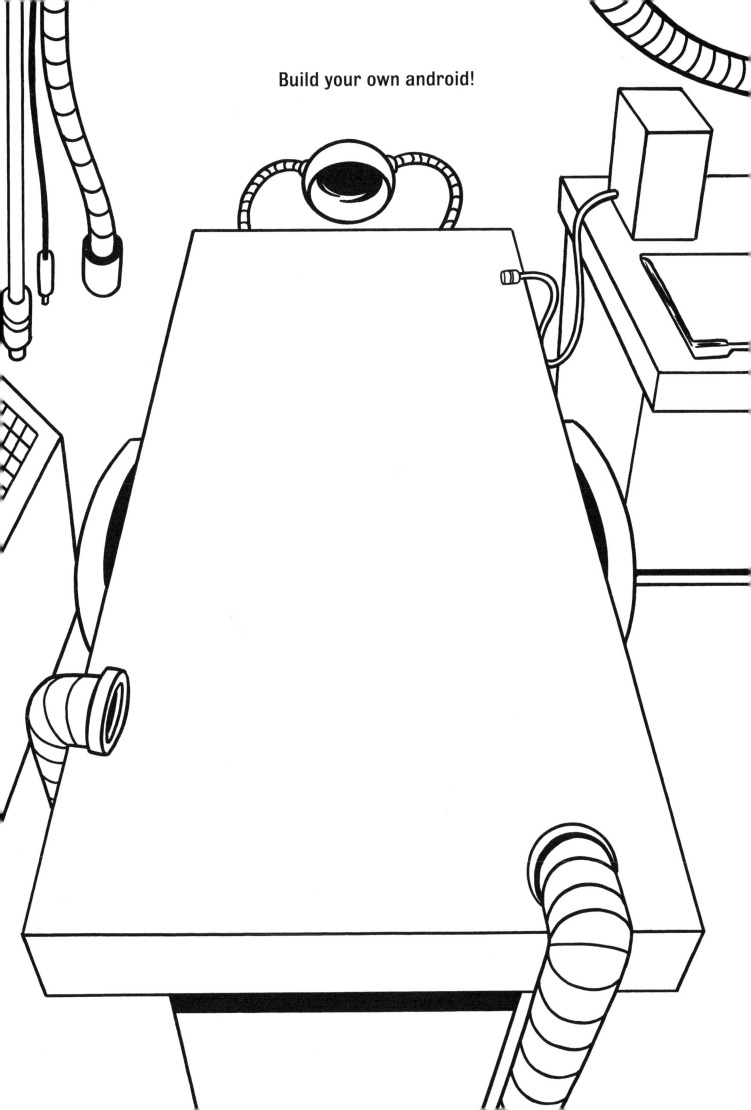

Amazo has absorbed the heroes' abilities and is using them all at once.
Draw the epic blast!

There's a break-in at the bank.
Who is stealing money from the safe?

The Flash foiled the robbery.
Put the criminal behind bars and
throw away the key!

Batman chased the Joker into a hall of mirrors.
So many different reflections, so little time.
Draw them all!

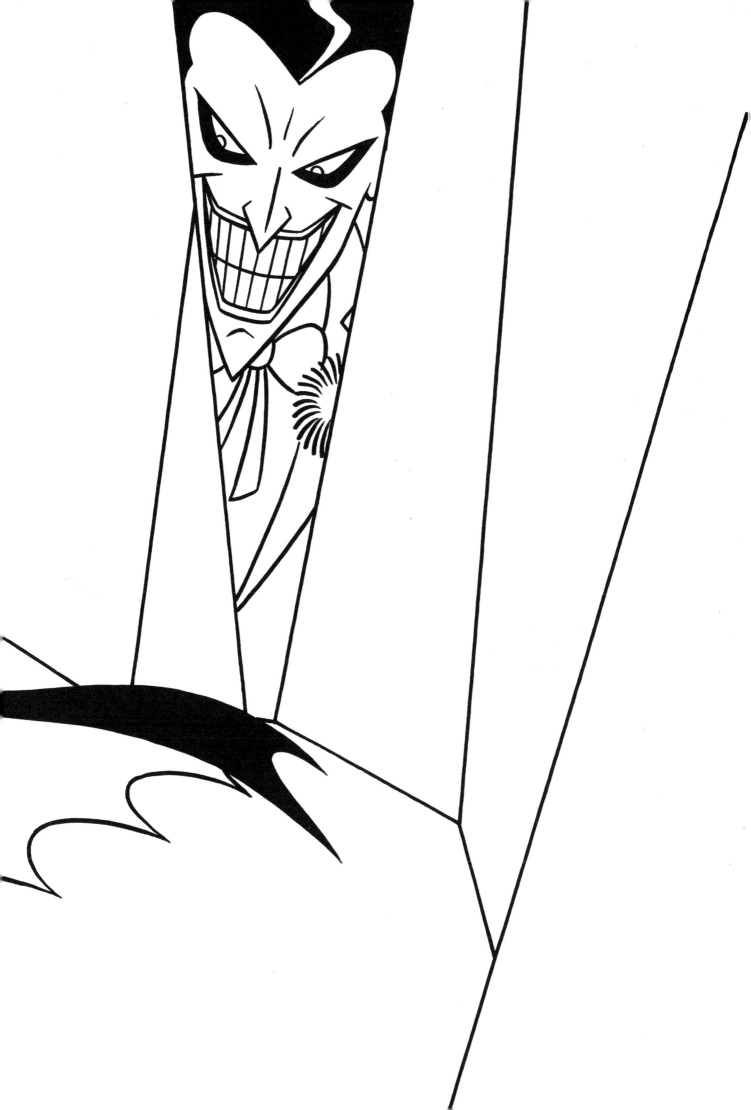

Solomon Grundy has tunneled deep underground.
Fill the hole and hide him from the heroes above.

Read all about it!
Draw the action-packed front-page photo.

DAILY PLANET

DAILY PLANET

JUSTICE LEAGUE SAVES THE DAY

This looks like a job for Superman!
Help the hero change into his costume.

The Atom climbs into a computer's hard drive.
Draw the wires and the blinking lights!

There is an alien invasion from outer space!
What do the ships and creatures look like?

Battle against Brimstone! Aquaman must extinguish this fiery foe
with a big splash. Finish the waves.

Black Canary and Wildcat sneak into an abandoned warehouse.
What criminal activity is taking place within?

The Shade can manipulate darkness with his walking stick.
What shadows and shapes can you create?

Copperhead has a tail that stretches several feet.
Finish the tail and show what it is carrying!

Batman zooms through Gotham City in the Batmobile.
What vehicle would you use to fight crime? Draw it here!

Doctor Destiny is on the loose! What heroes will stop him?

Martian Manhunter faces off against Brainiac in a battle of the minds.
Draw what each character is thinking!

Green Arrow traps Deadshot with a net arrow.
Draw the net falling over the villain!

What special weapons does Green Arrow have in his arsenal?

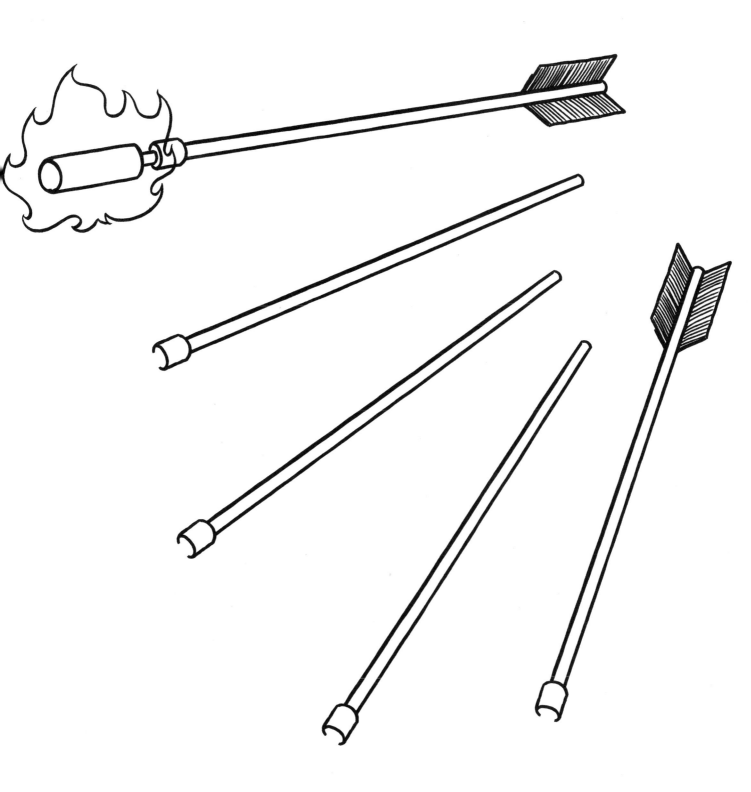

Doctor Fate needs help fighting off the evil attack of Doctor Destiny!
Draw Doctor Fate's Justice League friends.

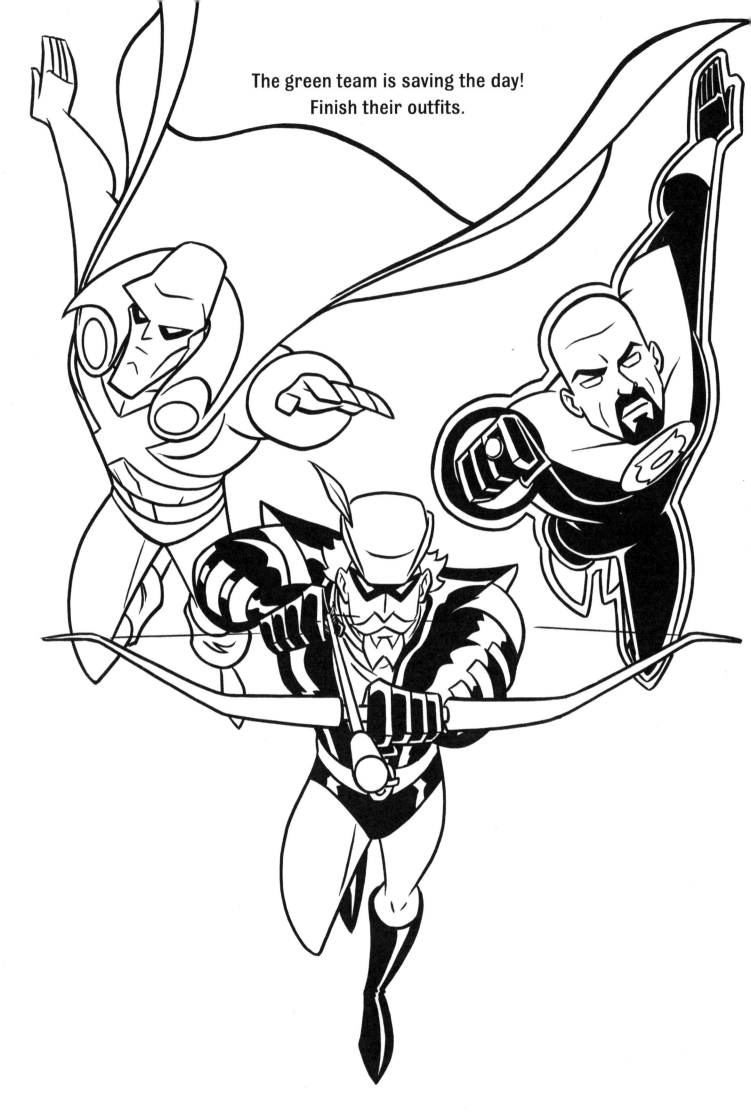

The green team is saving the day!
Finish their outfits.

Seeing red?
Doodle these crimson heroes.

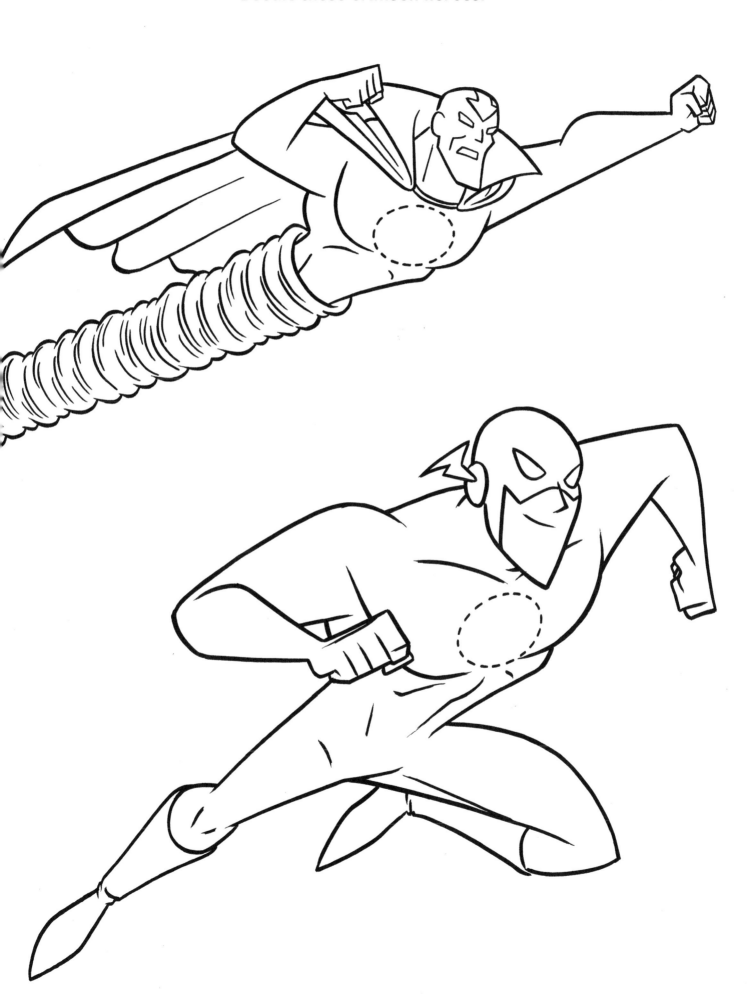

These heroes are missing something.
Finish their costumes so they can soar with style.

Superman uses his X-ray vision to spy on Lex Luthor.
What is the criminal mastermind up to?

Help Wonder Woman use her Golden Lasso
to reel in a runaway rascal.

Green Arrow's arsenal has some unique surprises.
Can you create some more?

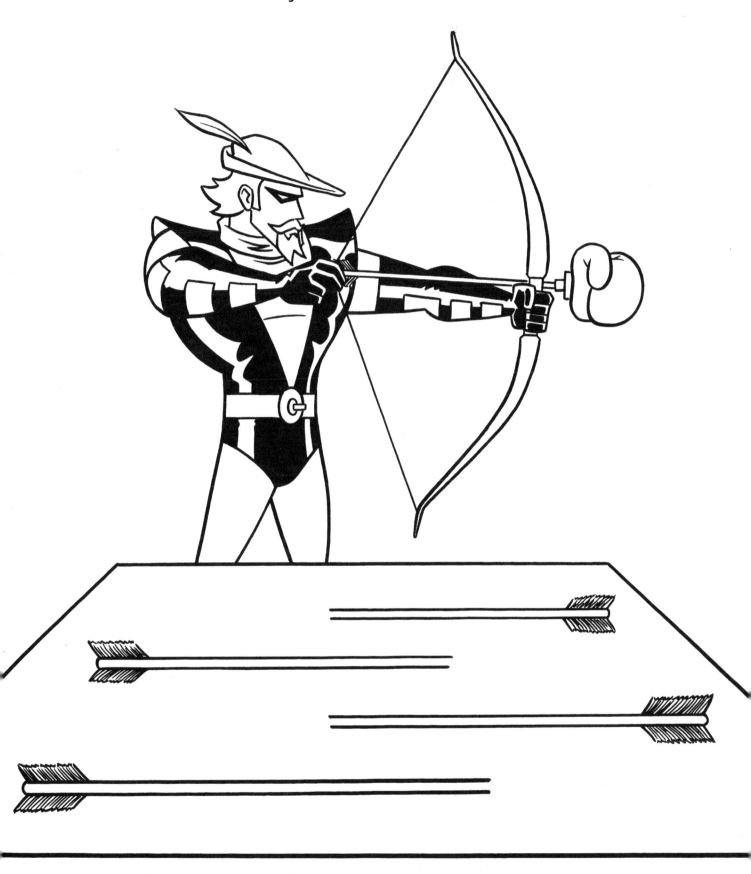

Amazo and Red Tornado are both machine men.
Draw the circuits, wires, and gears that make them tick!

The Justice League makes sure everyone is safe!
Draw your house and friends in the space below.

Create your own comic book.
Make sure to add word balloons and sound effects!